DATE DUE			
May 2'68			
GAYLORD			PRINTED IN U.S.A.

ETCHING

Etching

Modern Methods of Intaglio Printmaking

by Julian Trevelyan

WATSON-GUPTILL PUBLICATIONS INC.
NEW YORK

© Julian Trevelyan MCMLXIII
Pictures by Picasso © SPADEM, Paris, MCMLXIII
Published MCMLXIII in London by Studio Vista Limited
Published MCMLXIV in New York by Watson-Guptill Publications Inc.
Reprinted MCMLXV
Library of Congress Catalog Card Number 64-14768
Set in 12-pt Scotch Roman, 1-pt leaded
Made and printed in Great Britain by Staples Printers Ltd,
at their Rochester, Kent, Establishment

Contents

List of illustrations

Bibliography

New Ways of Gravure by S. W. Hayter. Routledge, London 1949,
  Panther Books, New York 1949
  Still the most authoritative book on contemporary techniques.

Etching and Engraving by J. Buckland-Wright. Studio Publications, London and New York 1953
  A valuable book covering in detail the whole field of printmaking.

Printmaking Today by Jules Heller. University of California 1958
  Another and more recent broad survey of contemporary practice
  with a lot of information for all etchers.

Printmaking by Gabor Peterdi. Macmillan, New York 1959
  Still more recent and most valuable and detailed.

The Art of Etching by E. S. Lumsden. Philadelphia 1926
  A more old-fashioned book, but one whose validity has been
  vindicated over many years.

About Prints by S. W. Hayter. Oxford University Press, London,
  New York, Toronto 1962
  Though addressed primarily to the collector of prints, this new
  book of Hayter's is full of things that every printmaker will
  relish, especially the accounts of varying workshop practices in
  France, Britain, and U.S.A.

Preface

It may seem superfluous to produce yet another book on etchings and intaglio prints when so many excellent volumes have appeared since the war. But most of them have been concerned with a much larger sector of the printmaking field. Of these, S. W. Hayter's pioneer book, *New Ways of Gravure*, and his more recent *About Prints*, have had a large influence in shaping the ideas of a great many contemporary printmakers, including myself. In America several good books have appeared recently, especially *Printmaking Today* by Jules Heller. In Britain John Buckland-Wright's *Etching and Engraving*, which was published about ten years ago, remains a work of the greatest value and breadth of vision, and I am indebted to him for a great deal of the information in the present volume.

What I have tried to do is to limit the field of investigation to the various methods of intaglio printmaking as it is done today, consciously omitting the historical background to most of the processes described. This is partly to give some unity to the subject. For there should be a single purpose in all good printmaking: to achieve by all the various means an eloquent and objective expression of the artist's own personality. It is all too easy in such a fascinating subject to lose the wood for the trees.

The development of printmaking has lately become so hectic that already, ten years after it was published, Buckland-Wright's book is strictly speaking out of date. Although he was aware of most of the techniques that have been developed since he wrote, he could hardly have foreseen the present huge demand for colour prints and the consequent shift away from engraving, nor the new status that etching has achieved. Doubtless before this book is out much more will have happened; we are in the happy position of living at a moment of great technical expansion.

I make no apology for publishing examples of the work of many artists whose names will be largely unknown. Most of them are past or present students at the Royal College of Art, where, as one of their teachers, I have been able to learn from their experiments as much or more than I have taught them. It seems to me that any school becomes quickly moribund unless there is this feeling that it is breaking new ground, and most certainly at the Royal College today this is the case. I am most grateful for all the facilities it has afforded in preparing this book.

I must also warmly thank all those who have allowed me to reproduce their work or provided me with photographs, especially the Courtauld Institute 9, 10 and 24, the British Museum, the Victoria and Albert Museum, the St George's Gallery, the Redfern Gallery, Madame Lacourrière, the Galerie Louise Leiris, and M. Dunoyer de Segonzac.

I am particularly grateful, too, for advice from Anthony Gross who read my text at an early stage and suggested many valuable alterations.

To Ronald Fuller I owe a special debt for his efforts to revive the almost lost art of mezzotint, the results of which are found amongst the illustrations.

To Richard Zimmerman of the Pratt Institute, New York, and John Paul Jones of the University of California, I am particularly grateful for the information about sources of graphic equipment in America as listed in the appendix.

Lastly, I am grateful to Miss Elsie Hebron for the excellent diagrams.

1 · Printmaking today

'Come upstairs and see my etchings.'

This old chestnut has rather had its day, and the image of the dirty old man luring the innocent girl up the ladder to his loft has lost much of its force. It may be not entirely irrelevant to inquire why this is.

The word 'etching' still sometimes conjures up an image of the little brown objects in enormous white mounts that used to hang in the hall of our grandfather's home. They were signed by the artist who had made them, and up to about 1930 considerable sums were paid for them at the Royal Academy or at certain London galleries. The best of them according to our present tastes were often technically interesting but not much more; of the others the less said the better.

About 1928 in this country there was a sudden slump in the etching market and many galleries refused to touch them again. Since then, and until recently, the word 'etching' has carried a slightly derogatory flavour to most serious artists, and even now when the position is much improved there is still a certain prejudice to be overcome.

However, the position outside England, and especially in France, has been very different. There etching and printmaking generally have always been treated more seriously. There was never any slump, and editions of etchings and engravings continued to be published and bought. But the chief difference was that, whereas in Britain etching tended to be the preserve of the so-called professional or specialist etcher, elsewhere the best etchings were made by painters who used the medium as just one other way of saying what they had to say. Pissarro,

Picasso, Matisse, Rouault, Emil Nolde – these are just some of the names of those who gave etching a new impetus and who discovered new possibilities.

It is only within the last ten years that we in Britain have woken up to what has been going on elsewhere in the world. Even now there is an immense ignorance of what prints are for, and before we examine etching and the various other kinds of intaglio printmaking we had better try and clear up some common misconceptions about prints in general.

First of all a print is not a reproduction. A print, in whatever medium, is or should be made and conceived by the artist himself; he will have knowingly chosen his medium so as best to express his idea, and he will have supervised its execution at every stage. In certain cases others may have helped him in the technical execution and printing, but his signature on every proof is a witness to his approval of each final copy.

Unfortunately, the issue here is somewhat confused by the recent appearance of a number of prints that are not prints in the true sense of the word. Several enterprising French firms have bought the copyright of oil paintings or water-colours by various famous artists, and have with devilish skill copied them in either lithography or colour etching, issuing them in expensive limited editions. These, of course, are reproductions because the artist never conceived them in the medium in which they finally appear. But to the uninitiated they are lithographs or etchings, and a confusion arises that tends in the long run to hurt the artists who have made their own prints. Hence it has become necessary to talk about 'authographic prints' to distinguish them from these reproductions which are really masquerading as prints.

The essence of a print is the edition. This can be of any size, but whatever happens each print must be identical, or as nearly identical as it is possible to make it, otherwise it is not strictly speaking an edition. In practice there are various factors that limit the size of an edition. For instance, the plate may wear out; also in Britain purchase tax has to be paid on any edition of over seventy-five copies.

More and more it is becoming obvious that printmaking should be considered as one activity, and the divisions between the various ways of making prints are becoming far less important. Already there are those whose prints are a combination of lithography and etching. Silk-screen and linocut can be combined with intaglio colour printing, as

12

we shall see. Moreover, we hear constantly of new methods of making prints that will not fit into any of the accepted categories. All this should be welcomed as a sign of vitality, and not condemned as it is in some quarters. The language and technique of painting has been through a rebirth in the last fifty years, and it is only to be expected that printmaking should reflect some of this re-thinking.

One of the important things to notice is the new uses to which prints are put. Those who buy them are no longer the collectors who file them away in drawers or who study them with a magnifying glass. Rather they tend to be impoverished young couples who cannot afford an original painting, and who will frame their print and hang it on the wall where it is expected to dominate the room with all the richness and authority of a heavily worked canvas. Prints are also bought by schools, hotels, and other institutions, where too they must be capable of holding their own in a large space. For such prints there is an ever-expanding market.

I make no apology for considering the demands of the print market in this way. The various changes and renewals in the world of art have always come about through an interaction between an outside demand and the intuitive answer of a few gifted artists who knew how to respond to it. The present situation in the print world seems an excellent example of this historic process of adjustment.

The chief effect, then, that this new demand has had on etching and intaglio printing generally has been to encourage the large print and the bold one. Even during the last ten years the average dimensions of prints have more than doubled. This in turn has produced new problems, such as the need for bigger presses and acid baths, and with the ever-increasing cost of metal, the expense of making an etching has gone up enormously. The colour print too has been much in demand, and just because previously little thought had been given to this branch of intaglio printmaking a lot of new methods have had to be evolved. There are those who say, and one has some sympathy with them, that etching is essentially a monochrome art, that the intaglio print in black creates its own colour and that it is a debasement of the art to treat it otherwise. However, it would seem that already the results would disprove this contention, and anyway it sounds suspiciously like the claim at the birth of the talking film that with the death of the silent film a great art was being destroyed. This may indeed have been so, but retrospectively we can see that something equally if not more valuable grew in its place. Time marches on. . . .

2 · Intaglio prints

Having now considered some of the problems common to all prints, it is time to examine intaglio and to define our terms. In practice we distinguish between the various categories of print by the method of printing in each case. Thus woodcuts, linocuts, and other varieties of surface print share the fact that they have all had their top surfaces rolled up with some kind of ink and an impression made on the paper either in a press or by the pressure of a hand, spoon, or other tool. Lithographs, whether on stone, zinc, or plastic are also in a sense surface prints, but the method of inking is different and the pressure has to be greater; consequently a special press has been evolved. The silk-screen or serigraph is essentially a stencil method of application of ink through a series of patterned screen stencils.

The remaining great category, the intaglio print, with which this book is concerned only, is printed in an entirely different way. Here polished metal plates are used, and the plate in each case is covered with ink. This is then wiped off clean by rag and by hand, leaving the ink only in the holes and channels in the plate that the artist has made. The plate and the paper are then passed through a press made on the principle of the mangle in which tremendous pressure is directed through felt blankets to force the paper, which has been previously damped, into the holes and crevices of the plate in order to receive the impression. The paper is in fact a printed mould of the surface of the plate, as can be seen by turning it over and looking at the back.

This much is common to all intaglio prints. The various categories that we shall be examining – etching, aquatint, engraving, etc. – are but the different methods by which the holes and crevices have been made in the smooth surface of the plate. Each has its characteristic quality and many of them are often combined in one plate. An artist uses them as a musician uses the various instruments of the orchestra to produce his music.

Most books on the subject give pre-eminence to burin engraving because it was historically the first technique to be evolved. Consequently it has acquired a *kudos* that I believe it does not altogether deserve today. As this book is largely concerned with the contemporary scene I propose to give the greatest emphasis to etching, which seems to me to lie closest to the expressive needs of the contemporary artist. Indeed it has so many unexplored possibilities that it would seem virtually inexhaustible as a field for technical discovery.

Etching, then, includes all the various ways of removing the metal and making holes in the plate with acid. At its simplest a coating of wax, the ground, is laid over the plate; lines are drawn through this with a metal needle thus exposing the bare plate; it is then placed in a bath of acid until it is sufficiently bitten to hold the ink. Afterwards it is cleaned, polished, and impressions are taken from it.

Tones can be etched into the surface of the plate by roughening it so as to hold ink when wiped. Aquatint is one such method of roughening the surface. Textures pressed into a soft wax ground can also be bitten into the plate.

Finally, whole areas of the plate can be exposed to the acid and bitten down to a lower level or even right through to the other side of the plate. This is known as open bite, and we shall see later what the effect is of printing from a plate that has been treated in this way.

So far we have considered only ways of making holes in the plate with acid. But there are other ways, sometimes known as 'sculptural', of attacking the surface by hand with tools. Engraving with a burin is the best known of these. Here the sharp tool cuts out and removes the metal leaving a 'V'-shaped groove which prints as a fine and distinct line.

Another sculptural method of attacking the plate is to scratch it with a tool raising a burr but removing no metal. This is known as drypoint, and an extension of this method, little used today, is mezzotint. Here the whole surface is scoured and whites and greys are produced out of the general blackness by smoothing and polishing certain parts with a burnisher.

Here, then, in a few sentences are outlined the various processes of intaglio printmaking. The rest of the book is a closer examination of just how these processes are done. There is always a limit to what can be learnt from a book, and the student or artist will no doubt take what he needs and discover the rest for himself.

Already it will be seen that we are deep in technique, and indeed any discussion of etching is apt rapidly to become lost in mechanical considerations. This is something that we have to guard against if we are not to lose sight of the purpose for which etching is done. Too many etchers in the past have been too clever by half, and forgotten that the medium is only a way for them to say something personal and significant. The imaginative impulse must sustain them through all the technical processes, and without it the whole business is not worth doing.

It is well, too, to realize that there are some artists for whom prints in general and etching in particular are too indirect a means of expression. Others, however, thrive when they are given just such an obstacle to overcome, and these are the ones who make the best etchers. There is indeed a degree of deliberation and planning that must go into the making of any print. And yet with experience and confidence, and above all with an idea that it is worth expressing, there comes also a kind of spontaneity that is difficult to describe. It is as if the acid itself was inspired. Certainly the most successful etchers develop some sort of 'green fingers', and the materials seem to work *for* them instead of *against* them.

The struggle with the various grounds and varnishes, the long waits while the plate bites or varnishes dry, seem all to add a special importance to the plate itself. And when finally a proof is taken and the result of all the labour and tension is first seen, the excitement for the artist is tremendous. He has in fact until this moment been working nearly blind, and here is his first opportunity of assessing the value of what he has been doing. Probably it is all wrong and he must punish his plate still further. It is in this way by successive actions of the artist on the surface of the plate that a print can become an image charged with the same weight and authority as a large canvas.

To realize the full possibilities of etching the student or artist has to acquire a certain *abandon* and attack the plate without fear of spoiling it. He must forget the cost of metal and of everything else. The more violent and spontaneous techniques that have lately become popular may help him to do this. But even in his wildest attacks on the surface of the plate he should cultivate a thorough and craftsmanlike method, laying, for instance, his grounds evenly; otherwise he will not achieve the result he is looking for. Thus experience and a thorough understanding of the medium are as necessary as they ever were. In the same way he must organize the etching studio so that the various processes may go on unimpeded.

This contradiction between spontaneity and deliberation, between violence and control, is one that runs through all the activities of the etcher. The spirit of Zen seems never to be far away.

16

3 · Etching

We must now consider in greater detail the process of etching, and to do this we shall try to follow through the simplest type of plate, a line etching drawn through a hard ground, from the bare metal to the pulling of the final proof.

The Metal

Etchings can be made on many types of metal. Those most commonly used today are zinc, copper, and iron. Each has its own characteristics.

ZINC. This has the advantage of being fairly cheap, and can be bought in polished sheets, generally about 40 in. × 20 in. There are various thicknesses of metal, but either 16 or 18 gauge is that usually used for etching. In the long run it is an economy to buy a guillotine that can cut the sheet into the required sizes.

Unpolished zinc can also be used and is cheaper. Pissarro did some of his most beautiful etchings on bits of roofing zinc, and some artists have used the back of old lithograph plates, but here of course the metal is very much thinner which makes it hard to handle. Also it may contain impurities which make the biting much more uncontrollable.

Zinc bites quickly and deeply and is admirable for most work, but since it is soft, plates with delicate work on them tend to wear down rather quickly. It is not used for burin engraving since it is difficult to control the tool in this relatively coarse metal. Also it has the disadvantage of discolouring coloured inks, especially yellows and blues, and so should not be used for most colour intaglio printing.

17

COPPER. This is a more expensive metal and is generally used for fine work, especially burin engraving and drypoint. It bites more slowly, and it has the advantage of discolouring inks less than zinc, and so can be used better for printing colour intaglio.

IRON AND SHEET STEEL. These are far cheaper than either zinc or copper and can often be found locally. They may not be polished, and to do this is quite hard work without some form of mechanical buffing machine. Some artists like the effect of an unpolished plate, and excellent etchings have been made on the backs of plates that have been already pitted by the acid. Iron etches slowly but well, and it will not discolour coloured inks; owing to its hardness it will not wear at all and enormous editions can be taken. Corrections with a scraper and burnisher are hard to make, but with patience and elbow grease anything can be done. When not in use iron plates should be covered with varnish or Vaseline to prevent rusting.

Cleaning the Plate

The plate is generally greasy, and before a ground can be laid it must be cleaned, otherwise the ground might lift. When water is poured over a greasy plate it will retract into globules. The cleaning is generally done with whiting wetted with a few drops of dilute ammonia and applied with a soft damp rag. Detergents can also be used to remove grease. When all grease is gone, water will be seen to spread evenly all over the plate; the whiting must be washed right off or it may lift the ground. Each time before a ground is laid on a plate it is important to clean it in this way.

Laying a Ground

There are two sorts of ground in common use, hard ground and soft ground. They usually consist of a mixture of beeswax, bitumen, and resin, and can be made at home (see appendix), but it is generally more convenient to buy them at an artist's stores, where they are sold in small round cakes or balls in boxes.

In this case we will lay a hard ground. It is not a difficult operation but it demands a little practice. Everything involved should be free of dust and foreign matter, the plate, the heater, and the roller or dabber, otherwise foul biting may occur.

18

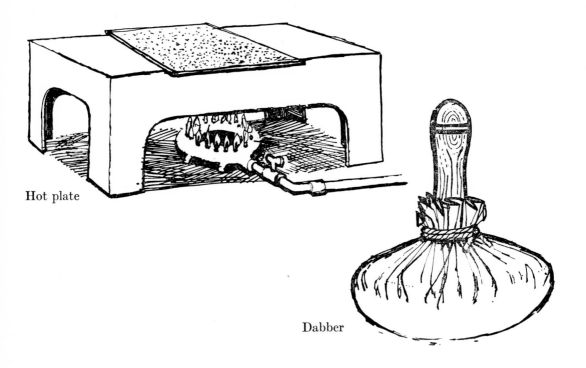

Hot plate

Dabber

To lay a ground we need some kind of heater. This is generally a sort of iron box on legs over a gas ring, but the top of a stove or a kitchen electric hotplate can be made to do. The plate is heated so that it is just painful to touch, and then a certain amount of ground is rubbed on to it, not enough to cover it completely, but such that it can be rolled out to create an even dark brown film. This is best done with a small leather-covered roller which should be kept strictly dust-free and used only for rolling hard grounds. The ground will only spread when it is melted, and a little practice will show the necessary pressure and heat to achieve an even spread. If the plate is overheated the ground will smoke, and it is then useless and should be removed with turpentine.

Another way of laying a ground is by means of a dabber made of kid which contains ground that melts through on to the plate, but this is perhaps a more difficult way of achieving an even ground. Liquid grounds from a bottle are also sold which can be poured evenly over the plate and the residue put back in the container. These are sometimes thought to be more brittle.

1 SHRUBS AND TREES. *Rosamund Steed*
  Line etching. Notice the differences of depth of biting

2 HORN PLAYER, from the Charivari suite. *Anthony Gross*
A recent print using a full range of effects all bitten through a hard ground. Deeply
bitten areas were carefully needled. Other tools such as roulettes and multiple points
were also used to penetrate the ground

3 LA BOURDETTE. *Anthony Gross*
An earlier print with great contrasts in biting, almost entirely made with a needle
through hard ground

4 ETCHING FROM THE VOLLARD SUITE. *Picasso*, 1934
A good example of the great force of his etched line

5 MINOTAUROMACHIA. *Picasso*, 1935

Perhaps the most elaborate plate Picasso ever made, yet all
needled in various bitings through hard ground

6 GHOST. *Valerie Fabian*
Line etching with aquatint. The figure was imposed in a second biting. Aquatint provided the tone. Notice the not unfortunate speckle of foul biting

7 SUMMER. *Ben Hartley*
A straightforward line etching fairly heavily bitten

8 LES BLÉS, illustration to Virgil's Georgics. *Dunoyer de Segonzac*
A linear tangle given form through Segonzac's nervous and elegant needling

Smoking the Plate

Before drawing into the ground the plate should be smoked, but this is not absolutely essential. Smoking hardens and evens out the ground and also makes it blacker so that the needled line will stand out more clearly. To smoke a plate the ground must first be melted on the hot plate. It is then gripped with a hand vice in one corner or along one edge and held upside down above a candle flame; this is best produced by three tapers that have been twisted together. The flame should move steadily to and fro across the plate, the taper being held about an inch underneath it. When the ground has been evenly impregnated with smoke, it is left to cool.

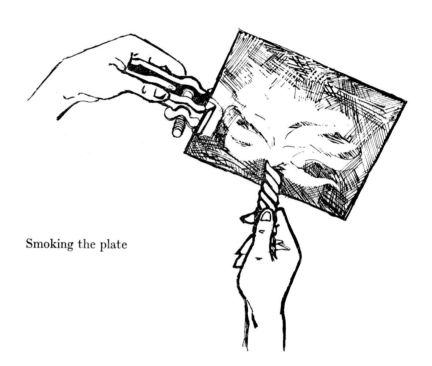

Smoking the plate

Needling

The plate is now ready for the drawing. This can be done with any tool that will penetrate the ground and each artist will probably evolve his own favourite tools. The etching needle is perhaps still the basic implement, but a pocket knife, a comb, a pastry marker, and an old door handle are things that have been used by various artists recently. Etching is apt to become hidebound in traditional practices, and is waiting for a breakthrough into a whole new range of tools; there is a field here for a great deal of personal improvisation.

The essence of a good needle is that it should flow easily; therefore it should not be too sharp, else it will cut into the metal. It should if necessary be blunted a little on a stone. It will be found that the best lines are made when the needle is held fairly upright, more upright than is the case with a pen or pencil. Also the pressure must be even, otherwise the needle may not have penetrated the ground at every point and such lines will bite unevenly. A yellow smear over the metal is a sign that the line is not clear.

The warmth of the hand, too, may smear grease into already worked lines, so that it is sometimes a good plan to keep a piece of paper under the hand while it rests on the plate. Some artists wash the needled plate with a little acetic acid before it goes into the bath to be etched. This removes all grease so that the acid attacks the plate evenly all over.

A little experience will show that lines in an etching are very different from lines drawn with a pen or pencil on paper. They have, so to speak, another dimension of their own which the artist will learn to exploit. He will find, for instance, that the various casual scribbles that he may get away with on paper, look fairly meaningless when etched. It is for this reason that shading and cross hatchings are generally discarded in favour of tones built from contrasting textures and lines. It is, however, dangerous to suggest any rules, beyond saying that it is a mistake for an artist to set out to reproduce his other work, whatever it may be, on an etched plate; he should rather try to let the medium lead him into making new discoveries.

The beginner is often apt to draw too little on his plate through fear of spoiling what he has. It is, however, far better to have too much than too little, and some of the most elaborate plates such as those of Anthony Gross contain an enormous amount of work which has all been drawn into one ground (illustrations 1 and 2).

Stopping Out

Corrections can be made before biting by stopping out lines or areas with varnish applied with a brush. There are two sorts of varnish in use in this country. The best known is asphaltum dissolved in turpentine, which is known as Rhind's stop-out varnish and is sold in bottles. This is a good tough resist to acids, but although it is labelled 'quick drying' it takes about an hour to become really hard. Thus to save time 'hat varnish', which is really shellac dissolved in methylated spirits, is often used. This dries in five minutes, but strong acid will eventually find its way through it and so it must be more carefully watched to avoid foul biting. Before the plate goes into the acid the back, which must also be clean, must be stopped out and also the very vulnerable edges. Here larger flat brushes that can be kept in the appropriate diluent, either turpentine or methylated, come in handy. In any etching studio there should be copious supplies of these liquids as well as plenty of rags and blotting paper.

The plate is now ready for biting in the acid bath.

Acids

The two acids most commonly used are nitric and hydrochloric. Each has its peculiarities.

NITRIC. This is used for both copper, zinc, and iron. Since each metal requires acid of a different strength, and also because chemical complications are set up where different metals share the same bath, it is important that each mix of acid should be used exclusively for one metal, and the bottle and acid bath so labelled. Nitric is a rough acid that is apt to enlarge lines rapidly sideways and not in depth, and it is therefore unsuitable for fine work. Also above a certain strength it heats the plate and tends to work more and more violently till it rips off the ground. But at the right strength, especially for zinc, it is ideal (see appendix).

HYDROCHLORIC. This is the basis of the famous Dutch mordant (see appendix) and when mixed with the right quantity of chlorate of potassium it provides an ideal bath for copper. It can also be used for zinc, but with this metal it is less controllable, especially with long bitings. In contrast to nitric it bites downwards and is therefore useful for finer work.

PERCHLORIDE OF IRON (see appendix). This is also sometimes used for zinc, copper, and iron. It bites slowly and steadily, but the plate must be put into it upside down so that the sediment may fall out.

28

This is a disadvantage as it is important to be able to watch the progress in the bath and to spot trouble as soon as it occurs.

None of these acids is so strong that the hand may not be used in the bath to remove the plate, but both hands and plate should be washed under a tap immediately afterwards. Care should be taken not to drop acid on clothes, and spilt acid should be wiped up at once. Mixing of acids should be done in the safety of a sink, and when disposing of old acid the tap should be kept running so that the joints in the pipes are not corroded.

Biting

As soon as the plate is in the bath the acid attacks the metal and the shining lines should go dark and eventually be covered with bubbles. The speed with which this happens is the best indication of the strength of the acid and of how it is working. If the metal remains shiny in certain passages it means that there is still some grease on the plate; nitric is better at removing grease than Dutch. On a warm day acids will work quicker; also it is well to remember that they get used up and need strengthening from time to time. Thus it is impossible to give rule-of-thumb judgments on how long a plate should remain in the acid to achieve a certain effect. As soon as bubbles appear, generally in less than a minute, enough metal will have been removed to make a fine grey line on the plate. Yet to get a dark strong line it may be necessary to leave the plate in the bath for an hour or more. In any case copper and iron bite more slowly than zinc. From time to time it is important to clear the bubbles as they inhibit the biting. This can either be done with a feather or by tipping the bath.

A line etching derives its 'colour' from contrasts of deep and shallow biting. Illustration 3, by Anthony Gross, is an extreme example of such a technique. To achieve this effect the plate is taken out of the acid as soon as all the lines are seen to be biting, and washed and blotted. When quite dry the finest lines are stopped out with varnish so that they will not bite any more. It is then put back into the acid, and the process can be repeated several times until only the strongest lines are left biting. But each time this is done, a greater time interval must elapse before the next stage in order to achieve the same difference of depth. It is as well to see that stopped-out lines do not reopen and start to bite again as they are apt to do, and also to watch out for the tell-tale bubbles on white areas which indicate that foul biting is going on. Foul biting is not necessarily a disaster, but it can come in the wrong place. Yet many of the accidents that occur to a plate can be turned to good account by a sensitive artist; to work *with* the acid and not *against* it should be his aim.

It is obvious that this process of biting lines of different depths can be done in another way. The deeply bitten lines can be bitten first and when they are well advanced the finer lines can be needled in. This has the disadvantage that it is difficult to needle accurately across already bitten lines. The artist must choose in each case which method is the more appropriate.

It is difficult to judge the depth of lines while the plate is in the bath; this can best be done when it has been blotted dry by looking at it against the light, or by probing the lines with a needle. The beginner is more apt to underbite his plate than to overbite it.

However, if he is satisfied he should clean the ground and stop-out off both front and back with the appropriate diluent, and polish the plate with metal polish. A flat paint-scraper is useful in getting heavy layers of varnish off the back of a plate, but it would scratch the printing surface if used there. Before printing it is important to bevel the edges with a big file or with a scraper so as not to cut the paper and blankets.

The plate is now ready for printing.

4 · Printing

The printing of etchings is a skilled craft, and good professional intaglio printers are now almost non-existent in this country. The skill comes in making each proof exactly like the others, and in doing so at a speed that makes the operation economic. However, any artist should be able to pull his own proofs, and it is not very difficult to get at least one proof out of three that is absolutely satisfactory.

A good printer organizes everything before he starts, checks his tools, the pressure of the press, soaks his paper (previously cut to the right size), cleans the press bed and sets his blankets right. His hands will soon be dirty and he will then have to handle the paper with cardboard or metal clips. But the hands of a good printer are never so dirty as the hands of a bad one.

Inking

A heater and a sort of raised box known as a jigger beside it are used for printing. Also there should be an inking slab which can either be made out of an old lithographic stone, a slab of marble, or a sheet of thick glass. The ink can be bought in tins, but it is more satisfactory and cheaper in the long run to mix your own (see appendix). This can be kept in a tin under water, and sufficient for the occasion put on to the slab with a printer's knife or a table knife. If it is too stiff, now is the time to add a drop of light oil; the consistency is generally considered correct if it will just drop off the knife in heavy blobs, but tastes here differ considerably.

The plate is heated and the ink is forced into all the lines with a big leather dabber or alternatively with a roller. It may be necessary to get it into the deepest lines with a finger or with a small piece of scrim. When not in use the dabber should rest in a saucer of oil so that the ink may not dry on it. When fully inked the plate will be black all over.

Wiping

The wiping of the plate now begins. It is as well to have prepared at least three pieces of printing muslin, tarlatan, or scrim, as it is generally called. This should be fairly stiff, but not so stiff as to scratch the plate. Each piece should be folded into a pad about the size of a hand. As this gets clogged with ink it can be shaken out and re-made with a cleaner part on the outside; when it is entirely clogged it will have to be thrown away.

The first wipe, done generally on the hot plate, will do little more than even out the ink and take off some of the surplus. With the second pad, and the plate now cooling on the jigger, it should be possible to get a rather muzzy image of the design. The third wipe should clear the surface ink off almost completely. The wiping should be done with a strong circular motion.

The lines, however, will not yet be absolutely sharp, and it is necessary to give the plate its final hand wipe. For this the palm of the hand is used in long gentle strokes. To clean the film of ink that is still on the surface it is a good thing to rub a little whiting into the palm which helps to absorb the ink, but loose whiting should not be allowed to get into the lines. The palm may also have to be wiped clean from time to time on a rag or on the apron. When the plate is absolutely clean and no black halos are visible round the lines, it is ready to go to the press.

The slight grey background on any etching which gives it much of its beauty comes from the film of ink that is still on the surface; the colder the plate when it is wiped, the thinner will be the film. Some plates are printed with only a rag wipe, thus making a virtue of the half-wiped texture, but it is of course difficult to make a satisfactory edition as each print will be slightly different.

In general it may be said that every possible effect should be etched into the plate and not left to the printer to realize (this applies particularly to colour printing). His is a skilled, but yet essentially a mechanical, job, and he cannot be expected to fiddle with the plate which would then become a sort of monotype.

The Paper

Any paper which can be evenly damped can be printed on. Papers with much size need longer soaking, and this is best done by immersing each sheet separately in a clean sink or bath for anything between five

9 THE THREE CROSSES. *Rembrandt.* Early state
Most artists would be pleased to leave it at that. But not so Rembrandt

10 Final state
Foreground figures have been scraped out, the horse turned round and given a new rider, and the thief on the right lost in the gloom. Not only has he increased the drama, but in re-working his plate so completely, it has gained immeasurably in richness and intensity

11 PLEASANCE FRYING TOMATOES.
Barry Kirk. First state
A plate made entirely by heavy needling stopped out and bitten to different depths. Already in this state the plate in the rack and the near hand have been scraped down

12 Second state
The background has been scraped to a uniform grey; the perspective of the plate rack and the cooker has also been altered by re-etching and the main pattern has been reaffirmed at the same time

13 Final state
A complete transformation in which Pleasance and the cooker turn round and look at us full face. Lost tone is replaced by aquatint. A trace of the lost arm can be seen in the much-punished background

4 DARK LANDSCAPE. *D. Wilkinson*

This plate was etched, in a moment of shortage, on an already worked plate, which had been scraped and ground down a good deal first. What remained provided a suggestive texture for the sky and foreground. The tones were mostly obtained by open bite and aquatint

5 STILL LIFE. *Alan Green*

A heavily worked plate that achieves its tones with a scraper and burnisher much as a painter might use a palette-knife

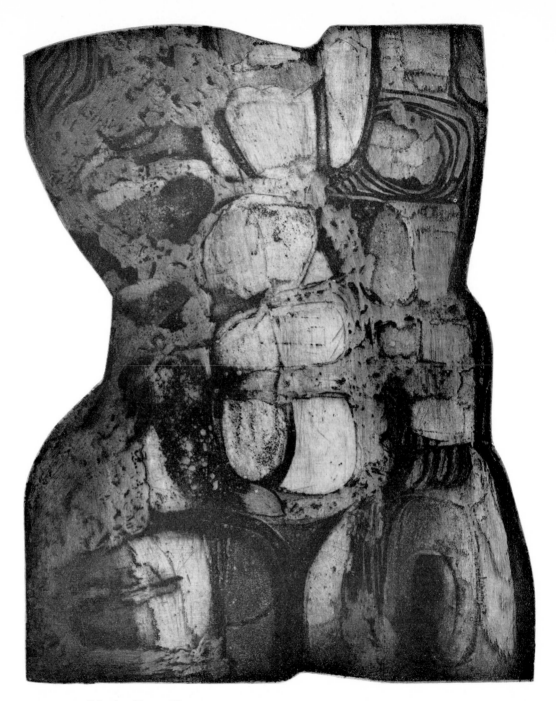

16 TORSO II. *Marita Poest Clement*

An etching by a sculptor. The plate was cut out (see Chapter 6). The tones were mostly obtained by open bite and aquatint. In this case the process went too far and metal had to be replaced with a soldering iron, chiefly on the left-hand side. The solder was then filed down and polished. This is certainly a sculptor's approach minutes and several hours, according to the weight of the paper and the quantity of size it contains. Waterleaf papers that contain no size need only damping between blotting paper and can sometimes be printed dry.

For proofing, cartridge or even blotting paper is adequate. For editions there is a wide range of good papers to choose from. Hand-made papers are always the best as they have a better surface, last longer, and retain their whiteness. Whatman, Crisbrook, and Head are the trade names of some reliable papers, but for those who can spend more there are many exotic and beautiful Japanese papers to be found. It is obvious that very fragile papers will not do for deeply etched plates.

When each sheet has been thoroughly soaked it is put between blotting paper under a large sheet of plate glass or thin zinc. Before it is used it should be lightly brushed to lift the nap so as best to receive the impression and also to even out any surface damp which might repel the ink.

Making the Impression

The press (see Chapter 9) has a metal bed on which the plate is laid. Sometimes this is covered with a sheet of thin zinc on which the plate and paper positions can be marked. The screws of the press should have been adjusted so that the pressure is even on each side. This is best done by passing an etched plate that has not been inked, with a sheet of blotting paper over it, through the press. Any differences of pressure will show up in the way in which the paper has been embossed. When setting the press for the first time it is best to tighten up both screws till they will move no further and then to unscrew them an equal amount on each side until the press runs freely with the blankets in place.

The blankets are valuable things and should be washed from time to time in soap and water to prevent them becoming stiff. They are of two kinds, the single thick felt that should be directly under the roller, and the thin 'fronting' blankets which come in contact with the paper. Generally a set of three is sufficient. They should be taken out of the press when it is not in use, and they should never be allowed to double back and pinch under the roller.

The inked plate is now sitting on tissue paper on the bed of the press and a sheet of damped paper is laid over it. Sometimes it is a good thing to put a piece of blotting paper between the paper and the blankets to stop them becoming too damp. The plate is now drawn steadily through the press, and when it is clear at the other side the great moment has arrived and the paper is cautiously eased off the plate.

If the paper tears either the pressure is too great or the ink is too sticky. If some of the lines are white, either the pressure has not been sufficient or there has been careless inking. If there is a sort of blotchy greyness on the print, too much water on the paper may have repelled the ink.

The proof should be stacked so that the ink may dry for a day, and then it should be redamped and pressed between blotting paper under light pressure so that it may emerge flat. The practice of taping damp proofs on a board to stretch takes away the relief of the intaglio and is not recommended.

After printing, all ink should be washed out of the lines of the plate with turpentine and a soft rag, and the back wiped, together with the bed of the press, the hot plate, and the inking slab.

Re-working

If the impression is only a first proof or first state there may yet be much to be done to the plate. The proof can be drawn on with charcoal or soft pencil and the next stage planned in advance. The plate can then be re-grounded and new lines can be drawn on it, or textures and tones as described in the next chapter. For re-grounding some artists prefer another kind of ground known as transparent ground through which fine lines can be seen; but this is not by any means essential.

It is rather a difficult business to re-ground a plate so that lines or tones can be re-bitten if they are not deep enough. The roller, however careful you are, tends to fill up the fine lines, and it is perhaps simpler to needle them again. Anthony Gross recommends off-setting a ground from another plate or even from a piece of paper in such a way as to keep the lines open. But the whole operation is unsatisfactory, and it is therefore very important to learn to judge the right depth of biting.

It is also possible that there are lines or foul biting or whole areas that need to be entirely removed. Here there are various tools that come in useful. A scraper, a three-edged tool that must be sharpened from time to time, will lower the surface and so eliminate a line. Scraping should be done from many directions round the point to be scraped; the area must then be smoothed with a burnisher and a drop of light oil. If a great deal of scraping is done the plate may become so thin that it will not print evenly. It is then necessary to hammer the area up from behind, and fill the cavity so formed with pieces of cardboard stuck to the back of the plate.

Scraper-burnisher

Lightly bitten tones and fine lines can sometimes be more effectively erased with a snake-stone and a little water. After the area has been worked in this way it should be rubbed with engraver's charcoal and water which takes off the roughness. Finally, after all these operations a brisk metal polish is required.

Plates that have been heavily scraped and worked lose some of their pristine freshness, but they acquire a rich texture instead. Quite drastic alterations can be made such as those made by Rembrandt in the two successive states of his magnificent 'Crucifixion' (illustrations 9 and 10). One learns in the end that it is never a good plan to abandon a plate at an early stage, and that there is always hope till one has gone through to the other side!

5 · An experimental plate

So far we have followed through the making of a 'line' plate in the more or less traditional method. But there are still many possible etching techniques that we have not seen exploited in any way. The plate itself can be regarded as a piece of sculpture, and the space it creates when printed as not just the illusionist space described in terms of classical perspective; rather it produces its own depth in which the various actions of the artist are recorded in spatial relationship one to another.

In order to explore this depth, and to discover in doing so various useful techniques, the beginner is urged to make an experimental plate, following rather exactly, but in his own way, the various stages as set out in this chapter. As each stage or state is completed he must take a proof, and he will probably surprise himself in the end by producing something far richer and more beautiful than he had ever conceived possible. This is in the nature of etching where the bud of the idea often flowers into something quite beyond the original conception of the artist. But unless the bud is there nothing much will happen.

STAGE I: *Soft Ground Line* (Illustration 17)

A soft ground instead of a hard ground is laid on the plate. This is done in the same way as with a hard ground, but it is not smoked and a different roller is used. It is important not to rub a soft ground which remains sticky and will take the impression of anything that is pressed into it.

A simple abstract construction is boldly drawn into this ground using such things as the point of a pencil, a piece of wood, and the edge of a finger-nail. It should not be too elaborate, otherwise there will be no

17 EXPERIMENTAL PLATE · STAGE I
Soft ground, line

18 FORESHORE LANDSCAPE. *John Craxton*
This was all drawn through a soft ground. The sky was etched in sugar aquatint and rubbed down heavily

19 EXPERIMENTAL PLATE · STAGE II
Soft ground texture, scrim

20 TROUBADOURS AT LES BAUX
Julian Trevelyan
This is essentially the same technique as Stage II, a line, drawn this time through a cracking varnish, and then a texture made with steel-wool scratched in soft ground. The tone in the sky is a coloured roll-up (see Chapter 7)

21 EXPERIMENTAL PLATE· STAGE III
Soft ground textures

22 CITY WITH A RIVER. *E. A. Dunn*
The river is produced from an impression of a piece of grained wood in soft ground, the city from an impression of an old newspaper matrix. Thumb impressions and holes through the plate complete the image

23 EXPERIMENTAL PLATE · STAGE IV
Aquatint

24 POR QUE FUE SENSIBLE, from Los
Caprichios. *Goya*
This miraculous aquatint is unique
among Goya's in having no etched
line to act as a guide

25 KAISARION WITH ALL HIS
BEAUTY. *David Hockney*
This evocation of Cavafy is
achieved with the help of all
the textures so far exploited on
the experimental plate, line,
swirl of scrim texture, impression in soft ground of old
printer's ornaments, and aquatint bitten to various depths.
On Kaisarion's shirt lines have
been bitten away in an irregular
open bite

26 RAMADAN NIGHT. *Taj Ahmed*
In reality this small print is in
colour, printed from two plates.
The dark tones are all aquatint with a minimum of line
work

27 EXPERIMENTAL PLATE · STAGE V. Open bite

28 ROUNDABOUT. *Tony Young*
An open bite *bas relief*. The whites have been
obtained by heavy burnishing

9 THE DOME. *E. Kempshall*
A strong design achieved with open bite reinforced with aquatint in the darks

10 DIVINITY SCHOOL, OXFORD
Valerie Thornton
A *cloisonée* effect achieved basically with open bite and much burnishing

31 LENINGRAD. *Julian Trevelyan*

A simple two-plate print, the black plate (zinc) being etched in various depths of open bite, while the crimson plate (copper) is registered to receive a texture of varnish dropped somewhat at random in certain areas

32 MIDI. *Agathe Sorel*

Here the relief in the plate is lightly etched, and the dark lines are made by removing copper with a scraper. The intaglio is inked in dark green. The relief is rolled up with a hard roller in blue. Finally, a soft roller carrying a less greasy brown ink is passed over the plate. It is repelled by the more greasy blue, and 'takes' only in the areas of less deeply bitten intaglio

33 FIGURE. *Brian Robb*
   This little print was made in the old technique used by Gainsborough and others of drawing in pencil on tissue paper over a soft ground

34 DANCER. *John Paul Jones*
   A delicately controlled open bite in copper. The drawing in asphaltum by this well-known American print maker had to be done very boldly and not retouched

35 FALL OUT. *Zev*
The splintered lines in this print were drawn through hat varnish, and aquatint was used to produce the tone

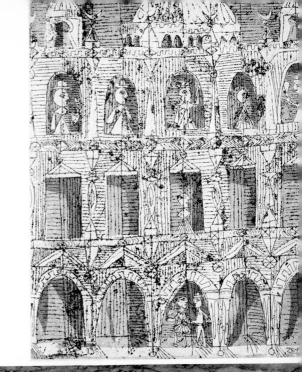

36 NORTHERN BATTLE. *Walter Chamberlain*
A combination of line work with open bite of various depths. Lithographic chalk was used to create a 'key' for the ink on the figures

37 ST MARY'S, LEEDS. *N. Ackroyd*
A good example of the positive use of sugar aquatint

38 MINION VILLAGE ON THE MOOR. *R. Fuller*
Lines were etched into this large zinc plate, and it was then heavily aquatinted all over. Afterwards the various tones were scraped out as in a mezzotint

LE CRAPAUD, illustration to Buffon. *Picasso*
A magnificent example of sugar aquatint, the know-how having been
provided by Lacourrière. Every line was drawn in sugar directly on to
the plate

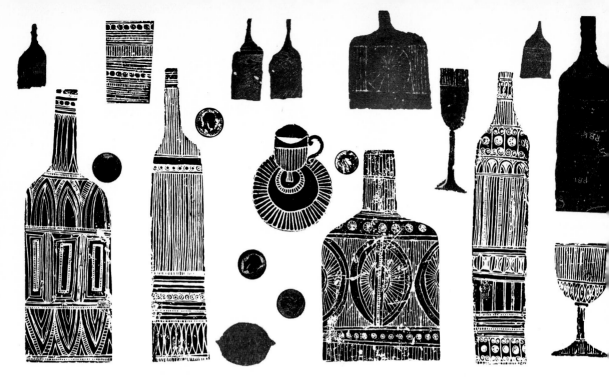

40 STILL LIFE. *Gerry Richards*

All the objects, including the coins, are inked and printed in relief in various colours. The objects are cut out by etching right through, all round them

41 BATS. *Christine Hodgson*

This print is really made from two plates printed in colour. On each plate the aquatint dust was combed and drawn into before being melted and stopped out

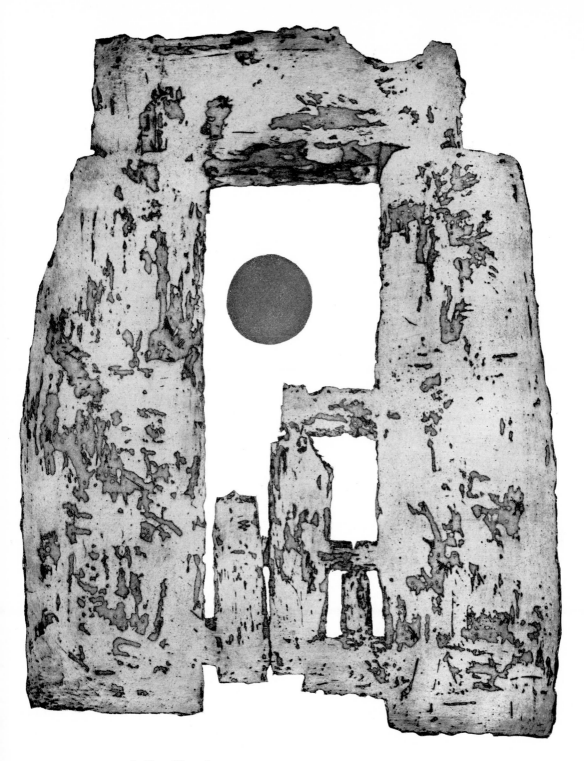

42 STONEHENGE. *Julian Trevelyan*
  The process of making this plate is described in Chapter 6

43 TOWNSCAPE. *Siriol Clarry*
This little plate, a combination of line and open bite, is shown here printed in intaglio

44 TRIPTYCH I. *Anthony Harrison*
This is a colour print that is mostly rolled up in relief, but in which certain parts are also inked in intaglio, while other more deeply bitten parts are left clear

45 TOWNSCAPE. *Siriol Clarry*
The same plate printed in relief

46 PAGE FROM 'AMERICA'. *William Blake*
Blake's Prophetic Books were all printed in relief and hand coloured by him. A method by which he could have produced the writing without drawing it backwards was suggested by Hayter and is found in the Appendix

room for what is to come next. Notice that if the ground is sufficiently thick the lines will already have a position in space on account of the furrows of wax that they throw up; where two cross the last to be made will seem to be situated in front of the earlier one.

The back of the plate is now stopped out, and it is etched in the usual way. A proof is then taken.

STAGE II: *Soft Ground: Wiped Texture* (Illustration 19)

Once more the plate is grounded, but this time the ground is vigorously wiped with a piece of stiff scrim or wire wool so that most of the ground is taken off, leaving the bare metal visible through a swirling texture equally thick all over the plate. This is now stopped out (preferably with quick-drying hat varnish) so as to leave only a couple of free shapes exposed. These, which cut right across the already etched lines, should not occupy more than a quarter of the plate's surface; this again is to leave room for future operations. Once more the back is stopped out and the plate is etched. It is taken out as soon as the textured parts are seen to be truly etched in. Nitric is best for the early stages of this plate as it removes the films of grease left by the soft ground better than Dutch.

When printed it will be seen that the 'colour' of this texture is interesting, and it will contrast nicely with the more mechanical tone of the aquatint that is to come.

A variation of this technique is a texture produced by rubbing the plate vigorously with a wire brush.

STAGE III: *Soft Ground: Textured Impression* (Illustration 21)

Yet again a soft ground is laid. This time various scraps of material are printed into it by passing it through the press with the middle blanket removed and a piece of paper above the materials to protect the other blankets. Various things will suggest themselves, lace, scrim, crumpled tissue paper, skeleton leaves, feathers, corrugated paper, and the imprint of a finger or thumb. Each will leave its own pattern in the soft ground. It is important to stop out the spaces between these textures and to impose them 'blind' on whatever is already on the plate.

Once more the plate is etched and printed.

58

STAGE IV: *Aquatint* (Illustration 23)

Aquatint is often regarded as the principal method of creating tone in etching. Here we see that it is just one of several methods. It has a rather mechanical effect but is none the worse for that.

The principle of aquatint is that the plate is dusted with powdered resin which is then melted into minute drops. When bitten with acid the plate becomes evenly pitted, producing in the printing any tone from pale grey to deep black according to the depth of the pitting. The simplest way of spreading an aquatint ground is to shake a silk or gauze bag of the powder over the plate, judging the evenness of the spread by eye. Big lumps or clots of the powder should be avoided unless a snowstorm effect is wanted.

The plate should just be visible shining through the dust. A plate that is too thinly spread will bite very quickly, but the aquatint effect will break down after a few prints have been taken. Too thick a spread will take much longer to bite, but at least the result will be more durable.

When the dust is settled the plate should be heated from underneath. It is useful to construct a sort of wire-netting tray or table on which all these operations can be done. A gas burner or taper should melt each piece of the plate until the yellowish dust suddenly turns absolutely transparent. It is as well to go round the outside of a big plate and to work into the middle, otherwise pools of overmelted drops will coagulate and the ground will be uneven.

There are various kinds of aquatint box in existence that will spread a mechanically even ground (see Chapter 9). The procedure with the melting is in each case the same. Much depends on the even heating and on the absence of draughts that might disturb the dust before it is melted.

With the aquatint ground laid and cooled two more free shapes are left exposed through the hat varnish, and the plate is bitten in the acid. Aquatint grounds generally bite far more quickly than lines in hard ground, and consequently it is best to use Dutch rather than nitric. As soon as the bubbles have covered an area there is already a tone; it is important to feather frequently. In this case it is a good thing to stop out one of the areas fairly soon and to let the other bite deeper so as to discover the different values of aquatint tone. Aquatints continue to get blacker and blacker until the pinnacles covered by the resin drops have been so undermined that the plate begins to flatten out again. The ink will now be wiped out in the printing and an uneven grey texture will be produced. It is important therefore to notice when this process of erosion begins, and this can best be done with a magnifying glass.

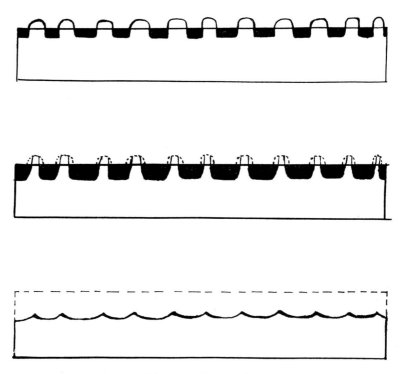

Diagram of aquatint

There are various other ways of producing an aquatint effect. A splatter from a toothbrush dipped in hat varnish is one. A speckled ground made by pressing sandpaper into hard ground is another. There are also various liquid aquatint grounds that are supposed to crystallize out into a fine speckle as they dry, but they seem never to be very reliable.

Aquatint is unsatisfactory for many reasons. Firstly it is fragile; on zinc at least it is very apt to break up when several prints have been taken. Also it is very difficult to achieve just the right strength of tone, and once an aquatint ground has been etched, it is dangerous to etch another on top of it to correct it; the best thing to do is to scrape it

60

right down and to start again. An even ground of the right density and a slow steady biting are essential if the plate is to stand up to heavy printing.

STAGE V: *Open Bite* (Illustration 27)

This time the plate is painted with asphaltum so as to leave three medium-sized areas exposed without any ground. It does not matter if they fall across already etched areas, in fact the essence of this experiment is the casual superimposition of one operation on another. The asphaltum is used to stop out because the plate will get hot with the sustained biting of large areas and this would probably break up the hat varnish.

In this somewhat violent operation nitric is probably the most effective acid. Clouds of gas will come off the plate, which should not be inhaled. After a few minutes the plate is taken out and dried. In one of the areas some spots of varnish or a couple of lines are drawn. The plate is then returned to the acid and is not taken out again until a definite edge can be seen on the etched areas. Once more it is dried and two of the areas are stopped out including the one in which the spots and lines were already drawn. Finally the plate is left in the acid till the remaining area has bitten right through to the other side. The plate is then cleaned, bevelled, and printed.

First of all the effect of the hole is dramatic—a white spot that leaps right out of the background. Then the deeply bitten areas will be seen in all their sculptural beauty with the ink clinging round their edges and their centres wiped nearly clean. In the case of the one with the spots and lines a complex new pattern is revealed, the product of a far simpler operation. Previous work on the plate can still be seen, but reduced and 'fossilized' by the action of the acid. In contrast to the aquatint, which is a surface disturbance, here we have patterns that have grown, so to speak, out of the very heart of the plate.

Open biting is used a great deal in etching today. It is a direct technique and there is an element of surprise and 'magic' about it which delights some artists, since a series of simple operations with a brush and varnish can be made to produce a far more elaborate set of consequences. With a little experience it is possible to foretell more or less what will happen, but to begin with there is certainly an element of chance. The bold etching of Kempshall is a good example of what can be done (illustration 29).

The first few prints from any area of open biting will be much darker than subsequent ones. This is because the bitten areas will smooth out with pressure and successive wipings so as to hold little ink. If a tone is wanted in parts of the bottom of an open bitten area it can be produced in the last stage of the biting by rubbing a little lithographic chalk over the parts that need the tone. A few minutes in the acid will produce a roughened surface to hold the ink. Similarly it is possible to make previously bitten lines stand up in relief in an open bitten area by inking them up as if for printing and then biting away round them, the ink acting as a resist to the acid.

The experiment which is now complete should lead the beginner to understand the real and essential nature of etching. With such an experience behind him he will be able to use to the best advantage any additional knowledge that he acquires or discovers for himself in the course of his work.

6 · Some other methods

There are a host of other methods of working, some of which have now dropped out of use and with which we need not bother. However, a few are used a great deal today and some mention should be made of them.

Soft Ground: Line Drawn through Paper (Illustration 33)

We have already described the effect of drawing into soft ground directly. Quite another quality is obtained when a drawing is made on a piece of thin paper or tissue paper laid over the soft ground. The pressure of the pencil will remove enough ground to give an effect, after being etched, of crayon or soft pencil lines. Gainsborough made several etchings in this way. It is worth while stopping out any large white areas before the plate goes into the acid because soft ground itself will eventually break down and produce foul biting.

Splintered Line (Illustration 35)

This is a simple method of drawing bold lines on a plate, not through hard or soft grounds, but through a varnish that splinters irregularly when it is needled. Hat varnish does this and so do certain other kinds of shellac. The effect when contrasted with ordinary bitten lines is often interesting.

Sugar Aquatint (Illustrations 24, 37 and 39)

The purpose of this technique is to enable the artist to draw in tone directly on to the plate and not to be obliged to paint 'round' each tonal shape. Goya in his remarkable plate *por que fue sensible* was not able to do this. He had to paint in his whites first and proceed stage by stage; it was like starting a picture with a highlight on the man's nose. But Picasso in his Buffon illustrations had been shown by Lacourrière an old technique that enabled him to draw his tones straight on to the plate, not with varnish, but with what is known as a 'lift solution'. The commonest of these is a saturated solution of sugar mixed with an equal quantity of indian ink. Others are mixtures of gamboge water-colour, black gouache, and sugar and water (see appendix). The drawing is made on the plate using the solution and it may be heated gently to dry off; actually it always remains a bit sticky. A varnish made of asphaltum diluted with an equal quantity of turpentine is then spread quickly and evenly over the plate, which is allowed to dry.

When quite dry it is immersed in water and the sugar solution expands, pushing off the varnish and revealing the design in bare metal. If it does not 'lift' easily hot water may be used, and it can be rubbed gently with a finger. An aquatint ground can now be laid and the plate etched in the ordinary way.

Many extensions of the sugar-lift process will no doubt occur to every artist. The essential thing is a new way of achieving a broad treatment.

Graded Aquatint (Illustrations 38 and 41)

Aquatint as it is generally used has a hard edge and a mechanical uniformity. It is difficult but not impossible to grade it so as to produce one tone shading into another. There are several methods.

One, used successfully by Ronald Fuller, is simply to scrape and burnish a uniform deeply bitten aquatint to the necessary tone. This is really the mezzotint principle applied to aquatint (see Chapter 8).

Another is to feather on acid while the plate is in the sink. With another feather or brush, water is built up on the surface of the plate and the two are allowed to mix and merge together. Saliva in the water is supposed to have a stabilizing effect on the acid. It is at best rather a chancy business.

Yet another method of producing a 'fade out' in aquatint is to rub lithographic chalk on to the melted ground, getting thicker as it approaches the edge of the area to be bitten.

Other techniques are concerned more with the positioning of the aquatint on the plate than with the biting. Christine Hodgson combs and pushes her aquatint dust around before she melts it, and it will be seen that this method has many other possible developments.

Rouault's 'Miserere' Prints (Illustration 47)

The history of this famous series of prints is strange. After the 1914–18 war Rouault discussed with his editor, Vollard, the possibility of publishing a series of drawings that he had made. Before he knew what had happened he found that Vollard had had these made into photogravure plates. Rouault was furious and declared that his designs were not finished; he proceeded to work on the plates themselves, which of course are just intaglio plates made photographically. He

47 NE SOMMES NOUS PAS FORÇATS? from the Miserere series. *Rouault*
   This plate, which started its life as a photogravure reproduction of a drawing, was
   worked on in various ways by Rouault until it ended up as it is now

48 GOLDFISH. *S. W. Hayter*
This dynamic drawing was made on a zinc plate, using a temporary resist which breaks down eventually in acid, so as to produce high relief lines (orange), in the same movement as lower relief lines that print dark. The intaglio was inked with a violet, and the surface rolled successively with orange (of a low viscosity) and green (with a higher viscosity). Each print may vary a little, but the same sculptural qualities of the plate are evident in all of them

49 MIRROR, RED AND BROWN. *Alistair Grant*
The rectangular panel in the middle of this plate was cut out with a cold chisel and
a hack-saw. It was inked in relief in two colours. The rest of the plate was inked in
intaglio in black and rolled up through various stencils in the colours shown

50 INDUSTRIAL LANDSCAPE
K. Armour
The lines in this plate were engraved with a burin. The fascinating 'marbled' texture is described in the Appendix. There is also aquatint and pressed tissue paper

51 RUSSIAN VILLAGE
Julian Trevelyan
This 'shift print' was made by inking the plate in black and printing it in intaglio, and then cleaning it and printing it in relief on top in another colour, but shifting the plate a fraction. The paper must be kept damp so that it does not contract in the meanwhile

spent nearly thirty years developing them in all sorts of techniques, many of which we shall never know, and when he finally allowed them to be published after Vollard's death there was very little of the original photogravure left on the plates. This is typical of the way in which an imaginative artist can create for himself a new technique.

Relief Etching (Illustrations 43, 44, 45 and 46)

Etchings can be printed in relief by rolling up the top surface, and this in fact was the way in which Blake printed his 'prophetic' books and *Songs of Innocence* and *Songs of Experience.* The whites in any plate that is to be printed in this way need to be deeply bitten so that the roller may not touch. A design with large areas of white is obviously unsuitable. A hard roller is required for the roll-up and the ink should be thin and yet stiff.

An example is given of the same plate printed in relief and in intaglio. It is also possible to ink up a plate in intaglio and then to roll up the relief in a different colour, but here we are anticipating the next chapter.

Cut-out Plates (Illustrations 40 and 42)

Here is another fairly new departure in etching. It is possible to build the image out of various plates in various shapes, using the white paper between as part of the design. My own 'Stonehenge' was made in this way. I painted in the shapes of the stones in asphaltum and etched away the rest for several hours in nitric. In removing the varnish with turpentine I found that at a certain moment it came away leaving the plate bare in the pattern that is visible. I seized on this accidental effect and dropped it in the acid for a few moments more. The sun was bitten in aquatint and printed in orange. The whole process was very simple, and the result was an enlargement of the effective area of the image by bringing the white paper around the plate into play.

Gerry Richards has made other experiments in this technique using a great many small plates. He is able to ink them up in different colours and to roll them up as well. In printing them he placed them all on a previously marked sheet of paper on the bed of the press. This he could see through the tissue paper that he used to keep the bed clean.

Before printing plates made in this way it is especially important to file the raw edges very carefully in order to avoid cutting the blankets and paper.

7 · Colour printing

Colour, as we have noticed, is in great demand, and the field is still wide open to those who can find new ways of using it. None of the methods which we shall examine is entirely satisfactory. In the first place the further complications that are added to an already complicated process tend to inhibit spontaneity; it is difficult to get excited about cutting stencils or tracing colour areas. But this is a problem that runs through all printmaking: the need to make colour separation more than a mere 'filling in' operation and to give it a creative function.

There seem three main methods of colour printing available; but each of them can be subdivided, and they can be combined in various ways.

Separate Plates

This is at first sight the simplest (illustration 31). Separate plates are made for each colour as in lithography. There are two difficulties here, the registration of the design on the plate, and the registration of the plates in the printing.

The simplest way to proceed is to make the first plate, print it, and before the damp paper has had time to contract, to offset the print on to the second plate. To do this it is easiest to place the print on the bed of the press and the plate on top of it. We now have the image in black ink on the second plate, and it is easy enough to delineate areas for etching in aquatint or open bite, using hat varnish or even sugar-lift. After stopping out, but before etching or grounding with aquatint, the ink should be rubbed off the exposed areas as the ink itself is an acid resist. If it is necessary to work through a hard ground, the offset should be laid directly on to the hard ground with one of the press blankets removed.

The plate is then etched in the usual way. In the case of an aquatint it is worth remembering that to achieve a full strength of colour, especially if it is a light colour, the aquatint must be a great deal deeper than would be the case if the plate were to be inked in black.

The plates are inked in the usual way as well, but it is generally convenient to use a small wad of scrim instead of a dabber, and, of course, separate pieces of scrim for wiping each colour. The inks themselves are ground in oil and sold in tins as copperplate inks, and they can be mixed on the slab with thin oil as required. It is also possible to print in colour using ordinary oil colours. For earth colours it is also quite simple to mix up colours from powder, but they should be ground for a few moments with a stone muller. It is worth while having a tin of copperplate reducing medium, as a little of this added to some of the colours makes them very much easier to wipe, particularly if they have been mixed with white, in which case they tend to 'scum'.

As has been mentioned, most colours become dirty when wiped from a zinc plate, and so copper or, better still, iron are recommended where strong colours are used. This does not apply to surface roll-ups which appear unaffected. In every case it is important to clean the plate before using with alcohol or benzine. It is generally advisable to wipe colour plates cold and not to warm them on the heater.

The printing can be done in either one operation or two. In the former case the first plate is printed in the usual way, but when it reaches the other side of the press the blankets and proof are folded back while the end of the paper is still caught under the roller, the plate is removed and the next is put in its place. There are various ways of doing this. One is to draw the plate position on the bed of the press. Perhaps a more exact way is to place two pieces of metal with straight edges, heavy enough to stay in place, against two edges of the first plate, and to slip the second one into the same position. Such an operation is illustrated on the jacket of this book.

Theoretically there is no limit to the number of successive plates that can be printed in this way. The only difficulty is that one colour may not 'take' easily on top of another while the ink is wet. This can be overcome if it is remembered that a colour with more oil or grease will take on top of a drier colour, but will not do so if the position is reversed. Thus in mixing the inks just a small difference in the oiliness of the various colours will ensure that they will overprint satisfactorily.

The second method of printing is to print one plate first, let it dry for twenty-four hours, re-soak it, and print the second plate. The difficulty here is to register the paper on to the plate, and it may seem easier to lay the paper on a blanket on the bed of the press and to place the plate on top of it, though the danger here is that the plate may warp.

It is worth remembering when making a design to be printed from separate plates that slight errors of registration, which are almost inevitable, become far more noticeable if the colour areas do not overlap. Thus, to take a ridiculous example, if space for a brown mast is left white in a blue sky, and if the mast does not fit exactly, a white line will advertise the error; the artist will be left wishing that he had simply overprinted the brown mast on the blue sky.

Printing from one Plate à la Poupée

This is a method that is very popular in France. The principle is that different parts of the same plate can be inked with different colours, provided the etched areas do not touch. They are inked and wiped with little *poupees* or 'dollies' of scrim. The difficulty is that the surface film of ink changes in colour from area to area and the result is apt to look a bit messy. Some skilful French printers contrive to run one etched area right into another and yet to produce identical prints. But I cannot help feeling that it is misplaced ingenuity.

This method is sometimes useful when used in combination with the separate plate method. Thus the first plate may be the key plate in one colour, and the second may be a supporting plate with several separate colour areas in different colours.

Surface Roll-ups and Offset Methods

Here is a huge new field for exploration. The most spectacular work in this direction so far comes from S. W. Hayter's Paris studio, *Atelier 17*, where he and his pupils perform new miracles every year. French inks are more finely ground than those obtainable elsewhere, and it seems easier there to come by the big rubber rollers that are necessary. However, even with our less satisfactory materials a lot can be done.

As already noted, it is easy enough to ink the intaglio and to roll up the relief, which is basically how Hayter's 'Goldfish' was made. To do this a big hard roller is necessary, otherwise the ink that it picks up from the intaglio will be offset on to the surface. By mixing a little lithographic reducing medium known as Tintex with the colour it is far easier to get a smooth roll-up.

A variation of this technique is to print the intaglio in one colour and to keep the paper damp under wet blotting paper. Meanwhile the plate is cleaned and the relief rolled up in another colour. It is then printed, but by purposely shifting the register slightly a very strange relief effect is obtained (illustration 50).

72

It will be obvious that the roll-up can be made to take a conceived pattern if applied through a stencil. This can be cut from a strong but not too thick sheet of paper which has been passed through the press, dry, over the plate, and on which the relief of the main design can be seen.

Alistair Grant (illustration 49) has used stencils and an adaptation of the cut-out plate method already described. In order to ink more easily in different colours he cut a square panel out of the middle of his plate with a cold chisel and hacksaw, and this he was able to ink with roll-ups and intaglio quite separate from the surrounding plate.

A further development of the stencil process is where several such stencils overlap. New colours are produced where the inks act as filters and these can be accurately controlled by the amount of oil mixed into each colour as already set out.

It is also possible to offset a design from a silk-screen on to the surface of a plate, and Hayter has experimented in offsetting from an adjacent linocut with a large roller which picks up the image and puts it accurately on to the inked plate. Great luminosity and violence of colour is obtained, but there is some loss of the three-dimensional qualities of the plate that we have admired. However, these are to some extent restored in certain plates that come from *Atelier 17* where after a roll-up in one colour with a hand roller, a second roll-up in another colour with a soft roller penetrates the depths of the intaglio; the second colour being less oily will not 'take' on the relief. The inter-play between soft and hard rollers and between stiff and greasy inks produces a huge range of possibilities where colours seem to exist in many different levels at once and to shimmer like the wings of butterflies (illustration 32).

It will be seen that much of the creative activity is here transferred from the etching of the plate to the printing, and some of the methods used do not lend themselves to the making of large editions. A printer might be reluctant to undertake such work, but it must be remembered that in France there is a long tradition of craftsmen printers such as those to be found in the print studios of Lacourrière who work with, understand, and realize the ideas of contemporary artists.

In this country with its different resources and materials it is natural and a good thing that in the long run other techniques should develop. Thus the making of colour etchings from separate plates may become our regional virtue, just as houses are built of stone in Yorkshire and of wood in Canada.

8 · Engraving – drypoint – mezzotint

We now leave the sphere of etching for the various 'sculptural' methods of making holes in plates. Of these the most important and the earliest is burin engraving. Indeed we are told that the whole idea of intaglio printing comes from some anonymous genius who decided to adapt the skills that had gone into the embellishment of steel armour in the latter Middle Ages to the new science of printing. Engraving nowadays is generally done on copper rather than steel, and since copper is the more malleable of the two we will confine our inquiry to this metal.

Burin

The engraver's best and only friend is his burin. With it he must accomplish literally everything; he will think, feel, and create with it, so the sooner he learns to love and cherish it the better. An unpretentious little tool, it is simply a bar of highly tempered steel, square or lozenge shaped in section. One end is cut at an angle of 45 degrees or a bit more to form the cutting facet; the other is set into a round handle, but the shaft should be bent just before it enters so as to let the handle fit snugly into the palm. On the whole burins of square section are those recommended for general use.

74

When the burin is first set up it is important that it should be properly sharpened, as this is the engraver's responsibility. Two stones are necessary, an aloxite or carborundum for grinding and an arkansas or similar stone for honing. First the bottom edge should be made sharp, and this is done by grinding each of the two undersurfaces in their full length, first on the aloxite and then on the arkansas; they should be held flat against the stone and rubbed up and down until the edge is felt to be really sharp. Then the cutting facet is sharpened by holding the shaft firmly between the fingers near the tip. In this position it is briskly rotated on both stones, care being taken to keep the surface flat on the stone all the time. A few drops of oil are necessary. The whole operation is difficult to describe and if possible a demonstration by a skilled engraver should be sought.

The cutting facet, but not the lower edge, should be constantly re-sharpened as the work proceeds. Nothing is so disastrous as working with a blunt burin. If the point breaks often the whole cutting facet should be ground down to a steeper angle.

The essence of engraving technique is that the plate moves and not the arm, so that to cut a curve the plate is gently rotated while the arm drives the burin on in the same direction. For this reason some engravers work on a leather sandbag on which the plate can be spun, but for a large plate a smooth table is as good if not better. There is no special way to hold the tool; the hand soon discovers the position of greatest control and comfort.

It is important not to try to cut out too much in one operation, and to keep the burin moving at the right depth where it does not get bogged down into the metal. If a deep line is required the burin is slipped into the previous groove and a further cut is made.

A sharp burin digs out the metal in a small spiral twirl as it goes along. It also leaves a small burr at the edge of the line which prints irregularly. It is best to scrape this off as the work proceeds, as also the little nicks of metal formed at the end of each cut. An engraved plate should feel quite smooth.

In order to plan a complex plate it is sometimes necessary to draw the design on to it as a guide. This can be done by tracing with carbon paper and in various other ways. Some engravers draw the design on with a Flo-master or other felt pen and then dip the plate into nitric acid for a few seconds, enough to dull the surface and leave the lines shining when the Flo-master lines have been cleaned off. The dulled surface is also less trying to the eyes and may be polished up afterwards.

Engraving is a slow and skilful business, and a plate takes a long while to build up. The beginner is advised to swan about on an old plate for some time until he feels a certain confidence and ease. Stiffness and cramp are signs that he is not holding his tool rightly. As well as lines he should try to build up tone, using shading and cross hatching. By pure hard work engravings can be charged with all the weight and sculptural qualities that we have found in etching. Indeed, metal gouges have been used to produce effects similar to open bite. Hayter himself has often contrasted a system of engraved lines with areas of texture etched through a soft ground, and other combinations of etching and engraving are not unknown.

Yet perhaps fundamentally engraving is a linear technique where each line is a living thing; it has been fought for against the resistance of the metal. It is also very sensitive to the personality of the artist and no two engravers cut alike. Joseph Hecht who worked in Paris and who taught Hayter was someone who made out of engraving just such a personal means of expression and who has influenced many artists since (illustrations 52, 53 and 54).

Drypoint (Illustrations 55, 56 and 57)

This is a much abused technique. Superficially it seems easy to do, but to control it and to produce with it a memorable image is far more difficult.

Whereas with engraving the metal is removed, in drypoint the surface is merely scratched and a burr is raised. The burr rather than the line is what holds the ink, and the peculiar feathery blackness of a drypoint line comes from the ink lying up against the burr rather as snow drifts up against a hedge in winter.

A drypoint needle has to be strong enough to cut into the metal, and so special heavy steel needles in steel shafts are generally used. Some artists prefer diamonds or sapphires set in steel.

Much depends on the angle at which the needle is held. When cutting at a low angle a big jagged burr is thrown up and consequently the line will catch a lot of ink. When being pulled straight towards one the burr will be small and the line will consequently print fine. It is important to remember this in making curves so that the wrist should make the necessary adjustment in order to keep the line even.

Zinc is such a soft metal that it is unsuitable for drypoint. Copper is harder, but even then the burr will begin to close down after a few

76

proofs. Thus drypointed plates that are to be printed in big editions need to be sent away to somewhere where they may be steel-faced (see appendix). They will then stand up to far greater punishment in the press.

There have also been attempts to make drypoints on Perspex and other kinds of plastic, but again there is the difficulty of printing large editions from such fragile plates.

Mezzotint (Illustrations 58 and 59)

This technique used enormously in reproductions during the last century is not often used today. Nevertheless it has possibilities that await exploitation by the contemporary artist.

Basically the idea is that the whole plate is scoured in such a way as to produce an even burr all over that will print black. Lighter tones from dark grey to white are then picked out with a burnisher and scraper. The laborious work of raising the burr on the plate is done with an instrument known as a rocker. This is generally a curved blade with a handle in the middle and an indented edge which is rocked methodically all over the plate in different directions till the whole surface is torn up. The work of burnishing, scraping and polishing then begins, and sometimes the design is lightly etched on to the plate previously to act as a guide. Local passages can be made dark once more by using a roulette, a small toothed wheel that restores the burr to flattened areas. Incidentally this tool is useful in creating texture through hard grounds.

Another more recent method of creating a mezzotint without a rocker is to submit the plate to the action of a sandblasting machine that is sometimes used in industrial potteries. This produces an evenly burred and pitted ground with great ease.

It is generally necessary to steel-face mezzotint plates before editions can be pulled.

9 · Equipment and organization of an etching studio

It will perhaps be useful to say a few words about the equipment of an etching studio, and also about the running of such a place, the prices of some of the items, and which of them are the most essential.

Presses

No etching studio can function without a press, though these are now hard to come by, and very few are being made. Presses can be anything from little table presses with a bed 8 or 10 in. wide to the vast geared presses with 40-in. beds that take up a lot of space and weigh several tons.

Ideally the length of the roller, and consequently the width of the bed, should be at least twice the width of the plate to be printed in order that enough pressure should be brought to bear on the plate. Thus little table presses cannot print anything much bigger than a Christmas card and are not much use to anyone. It is only from about 18 in. and upwards that presses become interesting.

The smaller presses are generally star-wheeled with spokes that turn the roller directly. Some printers prefer these because they can feel more easily the pressure of the plate. But heavier presses are generally geared. All the parts of a press, the rollers, the frame, the bed, are very heavy and need careful professional assembly and adjustment. Metal stops should be fixed to the ends of the bed so that it may not accidentally be pushed out from between the rollers and crash on to the floor or on to somebody's foot; bad accidents can happen in this way.

Since the maximum pressure should be brought to bear in printing any plate, it is important that it should be placed along the length of the bed and not across it.

Current prices for presses vary from about £20 or £30 for table presses to about £1,000 for the largest sizes. Second-hand and reconditioned presses are sometimes to be found.

Aquatint Boxes

These can be of many kinds.

A big hat-box with a hole near the bottom through which a bellows can blow up a cloud of dust has been successfully used. The same principle applied to a sort of big home-made cupboard with a grid half-way up, on to which the plate is slid, would seem more efficient.

The more elaborate varieties include those that have revolving shutters that kick up the dust, and even boxes that work with electric fans.

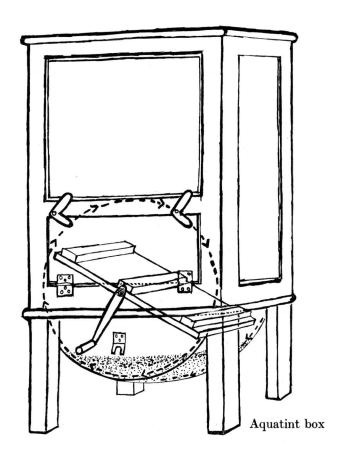

Aquatint box

79

Acid Baths

There are now a good many plastic acid baths available that are far safer than the porcelain or glass varieties. The biggest are even supplied with screw-in draining cocks in the corners.

A home-made method of etching large plates is to make the plate itself into a bath by erecting plasticine walls around the edge. There are obvious difficulties here in handling the acid, and the walls have an unfortunate tendency to leak. But many good plates have been made in this way.

Plastic baths range from £20 for the biggest to about £2 for the smallest.

Fume Extractors

Any etching studio where a great deal of etching is done, such as one in an art school, should seriously consider whether a fume extractor over the acid baths is not necessary. Modern techniques of open biting can liberate a very great quantity of gas, chlorine in the case of hydrochloric acid, and nitric oxide in the case of copper in nitric. This can be dangerous when breathed in, and its mere presence in the room will corrode metals.

Extractors are generally fitted by laboratory equipment makers, and they should include a fan to suck out the fumes into a duct leading out of the building. It is important that the cover should not make it awkward or difficult to get at the baths, and it should not exclude the light. Unfortunately extractors tend to be rather expensive to install.

If it is impossible to build one, the acid bath area should at least be as separate and well ventilated as possible. It goes without saying that the proximity of a sink is important, as no one in their senses would want to drop acid about the room when taking a plate out of the bath.

Tools

Burnishers, burins, scrapers and rollers have already been described. It is important that they should be kept in good condition. Rollers, for instance, should be kept hanging up and periodically cleaned, and it is a major crime to work on a plate in the bath with a scraper, needle, or worst of all burnisher; the acid will destroy the surface immediately.

There are various kinds of needle on sale, one being a plastic needle-holder into which gramophone needles can be inserted. A favourite old penknife can become a very good instrument for drawing on a plate, and steel combs for making multiple lines also come in handy. A big file, a small hammer for punching the backs of plates, and a small metal saw are also useful things to have.

Organization

It is impossible to do more than to stress a few factors that are important in arranging any etching studio. Thus acid baths should be near a sink and working tables should face the light, as only so can needling be properly seen. This is also a good position for engraving. Adequate light is very important, especially where fine work is done.

It is a good plan to have a special dirty corner for removing grounds and varnishes. Some artists recommend a large tray of sawdust for this purpose that can be rubbed over the plates when they have been soaked in diluent. Another table should be set aside for backing plates and stopping out, with space to lean them while drying. Aquatint operations, especially if they are of the shaken bag variety, should be conducted in a draught-free corner.

It is important when planning the printing area to account for the full extension of the bed of the press in either direction, and to leave space at each end to handle the plates. There should be enough table area available to lay out several proofs and to house a good stack of soaked paper.

Heaters and jiggers are easiest to work on when the top surfaces are 3 ft. 6 in. from the ground. Cupboards and drawers are of course essential for storage, and special care should be taken to store acids safely.

Dirt is, of course, a great problem. It accumulates everywhere, on tables, chairs, heaters, jiggers, and the handles of presses become quickly encrusted. A professional printer is able to keep things more or less in control, but in the atmosphere of an art school it becomes very difficult. All that can be suggested is that each day after work the essential things are cleaned, and these include heaters, jiggers, press beds, and ink slabs. It is useful, too, to have a cleaning outfit for the hands such as is common in garages and factories. A dollop of cleansing liquid is dispensed from a small container each time the hand presses it and the hands are then washed in hot water with a scrubbing brush and dried on paper tissues. An etcher's hands become easily ingrained with acid and ink, and there is little that he can do about it; dirty hands are his trade mark. Some proprietary barrier creams may help a little, and certain operations, but not printing, can be performed in rubber gloves.

It is a good thing to have handy a simple first aid box with bandages and plaster and remedies for burns. In the case of someone overcome with acid fumes the best treatment is a glass of water and bicarbonate of soda. Ammonia will neutralize spilt acid and so will washing soda. There are certain operations where there is a danger of fire, particularly where methylated spirits are used to clean the backs of plates which may then be heated on a hot plate. For this reason petroleum or benzine, both with a lower flash-point, are not recommended, though they are excellent diluents.

What can be dispensed with

This tremendous list of tools and materials may frighten the would-be etcher from ever starting. It is, however, important to keep a sense of proportion. Rembrandt and Goya, for instance, worked with the most miserable materials and had to improvise a great deal to achieve what they did. It is certainly true that etching as it is done today seems to demand a good deal more equipment. In Britain art schools are generally the best etching studios that exist, and there are many artists who would be unable to work if it were not for them.

It is almost impossible to etch without the fairly constant use of a press, even though a proof on plaster can be taken without one (see appendix). However, those who do engravings and drypoints are in the happy position of needing far less equipment, and they can take their plates to a press as needed.

If some economy is inevitable it has been suggested that stoves or domestic heaters can replace hot plates, though the grounding of big plates in this way becomes difficult. Aquatint boxes are really something of a luxury, but home-made acid baths are more trouble than they are worth and it is a false economy to try and save on rollers and scrim.

Editions

It is important, as we have noted, that every print of an edition should be as like every other print as it is humanly possible to make it.

82

Also it is important that the margins should be kept absolutely clean. Dealers are quite right to insist on these points.

When the artist is satisfied the usual practice is for him to sign in pencil under the print edge on the left the number of the particular print and the number of prints in the edition. His own signature should be on the right and if there is a title it should go in between. If, for instance, he decides to make an edition of fifty, he may prefer to print only twenty to see how they sell. Then if they are needed he can print the rest. But he should keep a print by him to see that the next lot is the same, and he should note the composition of his colours.

He is generally allowed to print five proofs beyond the edition that he can sign as artist's proofs. After this in order to show his good faith to those who have bought his prints he should score the plate so that it may not be printed again.

In old days there was a market for old plates and for early states of an artist's etchings, but such an interest seems to have disappeared. Yet if only for his own sake he should keep the various states of a print, for they provide a living record of the evolution of his idea through to its final embodiment. Also it is most important that he should keep a record of each plate and the number of prints of each edition. Without such a rudimentary discipline a gallery may well be discouraged from handling his work.

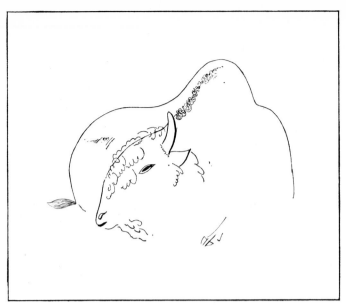

52 BISON. *Joseph Hecht*

An engraving of concentrated simplicity, in which each line is made to sing

53 QUARRY. *Joseph Hecht*

An engraving carried much further, where the cuts of the burin are made to suggest all the complicated textures of cut stone, broken ground, and distant forest and sky

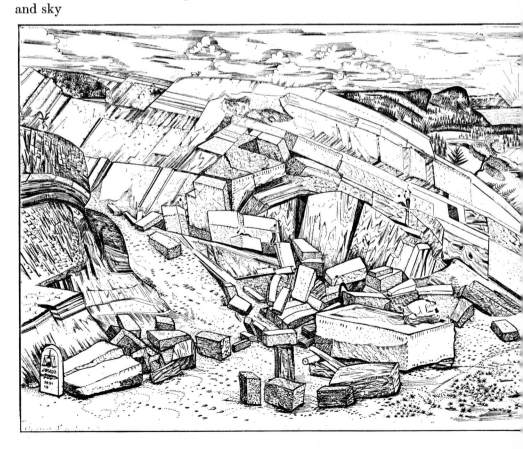

54 DEATH BY WATER. *S. W. Hayter*

One of Hayter's spatial explorations with a burin in several dimensions at once. The white rings are deeply cut trenches heavily burnished, from which the ink can be easily removed before printing

56 LABOURS DE LA VIGNE, illustration to Virgil's Georgics. *Dunoyer de Segonzac*

This, like Plate 8, of the same series, is really an etching. But Segonzac scratched so hard with his needle that in certain plates he raised a burr that remained under the hard ground during the process of etching, and was then immortalized by the steel-facing

55 PAYSAGE. *Valentine Prax*

The soft tones of this drypoint produce something very atmospheric

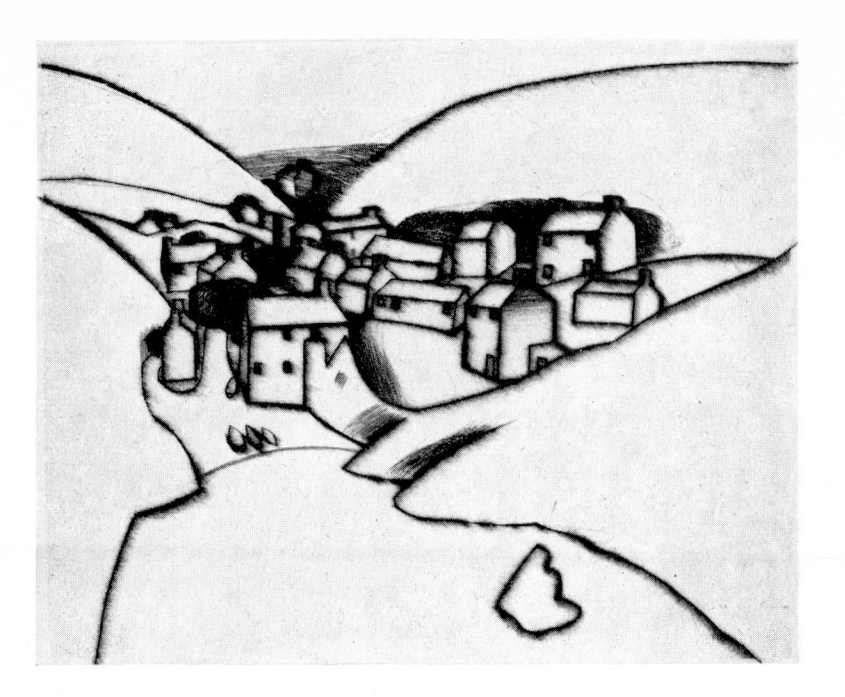

57 PORTLOE, CORNWALL. *R. Fuller*
A good example of the soft burred line of a dry-point

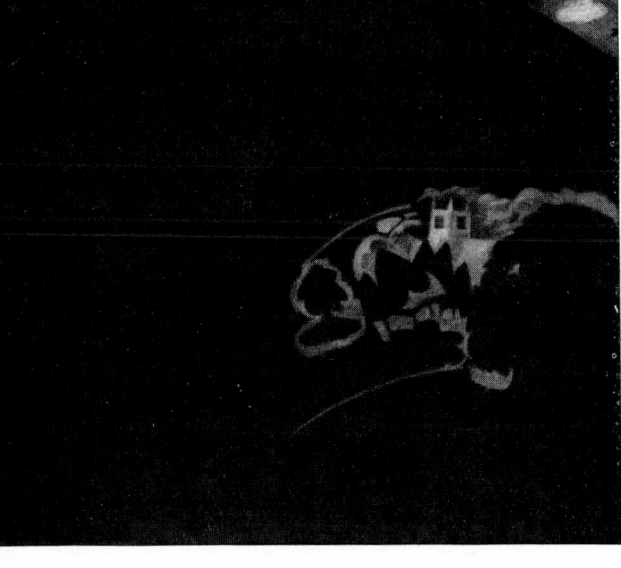

58 & 59 ST NEOT. *R. Fuller*
The ground for this mezzotint was laboriously made with a rocker. Some of the tones taken out in the first state were put back with a roulette. In the sky the marks of the rocker can just be seen

60 KING AND QUEEN. *Julian Trevelyan*
This etched mural, mounted on a panel 6 ft. × 4 ft., is described in Chapter 10

10 · Etched murals

This chapter describes a personal experiment that I have made which, strictly speaking, is not relevant to the making of prints, but since it grew directly out of my work as an etcher I may as well explain it here.

I had long been fascinated by the qualities of the zinc plates themselves, especially those from which editions had been printed and which stood in racks around my studio. The relief which had seen so much inking and wiping now sparkled as never before, while the hollows retained here and there traces of the colours that had once filled them. Sometimes I felt that those sculptural qualities that I had been searching for in my prints were more fully realized in the plates themselves, and this was confirmed for me when various friends begged me to give them my used plates as decorative objects to have around the house.

Why not, I then thought, produce plates that are specially designed as mural decorations? The occasion soon presented itself in the form of an exhibition of the Society of Mural Painters in the Victoria and Albert Museum, where all members were urged to evolve new mural techniques so as to tempt architects into employing artists more than they had heretofore. The 'King and Queen' (illustration 60) was the result of my experiments.

The two figures were etched on various sheets of zinc which in this case I cut to shape by long immersion in the acid bath. They fitted on to a panel 6 ft. × 4 ft. which I painted a flat olive green, and in this case I screwed them on through holes drilled in the eyes of the unfortunate monarchs and in other concealed corners. They were then inked in black and allowed to dry before being polished and glazed with a protective and transparent plastic varnish to prevent corrosion.

The effect of such a 'mural' can be very striking since the relief surfaces act as a mirror reflecting alternating lights and shades as the observer moves about. Such a surface can be a useful foil to far greater areas of non-reflecting texture such as brick, concrete, or plaster.

As a result of the mural exhibition I was commissioned by the architects of the new P. & O. liner, S.S. *Canberra*, to design and execute four large panels at the head of four separate flights of stairs. These were to be inlaid into a dark African polished wood.

Work on such a scale created new problems, and the entire etching studio of the Royal College of Art was littered with innumerable large and small pieces of etched zinc for many weeks. In this case I had my shapes cut on a metal band-saw, and the pieces were finally fixed into their pre-cut positions in the wood with one of those plastic glues that sticks anything to anything. In some ways I feel that the polished wood background was of too rich a texture for my mural whose sculptural qualities would have told better on a flat surface. But otherwise the effect was much as I had hoped.

So far this has been the extent of my experience with etched murals but there seem to me to be several problems yet to explore.

In the first place there is the question of scale. On a larger scale it might be necessary to use a thicker metal so as to achieve a proportionately deeper relief. Here aluminium might have certain advantages. Aluminium etches easily in nitric acid, but there is a graininess in its structure that is revealed once the surface is broken. For this reason it is difficult to control the speed and depth of biting, and stopping-out on the bitten surfaces is well nigh impossible.

There is also the opportunity of inking different parts of the intaglio in different colours, though here again to me it would seem redundant as there is already such a variety of colour in the ever-changing reflections of the outside world in the relief.

Another possibility to be explored is the superimposition of metal on metal, the excrescences being stuck either with solder or welded in other ways. In fact the line of demarcation between the metal sculptor and the etcher can easily become very thin, as indeed it should in an age such as ours of vast technological expansion.

Appendix

Acids

NITRIC. Nitric acid is usually sold in this country at 40% strength. When mixing, the acid should be poured into a measuring glass containing the right amount of water, and not the other way round. All this should take place in a sink, because heat is generated and there is the danger that the glass may crack.

For copper the acid, as bought, is mixed with the same amount of water.

For zinc the proportion is 1 of acid to 3 of water.

For iron the strength is the same as for copper.

DUTCH. Dutch mordant for copper is made by boiling 4 parts of potassium chlorate in a little water and adding the solution to 70 parts of water and 20 parts of hydrochloric acid.

For zinc 2 parts of potassium chlorate, 80 of water and 10 of hydrochloric are used, but it is not a satisfactory acid for most zinc as sold in this country.

PERCHLORIDE OF IRON. This is generally sold by chemists at 20% strength which is too low for most work. A strength of 25% or 30% is recommended and these can be obtained from certain chemical suppliers.

It is important to remember that acids need re-strengthening as they get used up and that they work better when slightly warm.

Hard Ground

There are various recipes for hard ground. Here is Buckland-Wright's: 'Two parts beeswax, two parts bitumen, and one part colophon resin. The bitumen and resin should be well powdered and mixed, and added slowly to the melted wax while stirring in a container over the gas. When thoroughly melted and mixed it can be poured into water and moulded into balls.'

Sennefelder's is as follows: 'Beeswax 12 parts, mastic 6 parts, asphaltum 4 parts, resin (shellac) 2 parts, tallow 1 part. Melt ingredients in an iron pot until they are all assimilated. Allow the mixture to burn until one-third is consumed. Cool and shape as desired.'

91

Inks

A good way of making black ink is to mix one part of Frankfort black with two parts of French black. It should be ground on a slab with a muller with a little medium copper-plate oil or equal quantities of light and heavy oil until the desired consistency is achieved.

There is a limit to the quantity that can be ground at one time. It can be kept in a jar or tin under water. It matures into a slightly warm black when it is dry; ink takes many months to become absolutely dry, though it dries superficially on a print in twenty-four hours.

Some artists like a mixture of copper-plate and raw linseed oil which gives a golden glow to the ink when dry.

Sugar-Lift Solution

Sugar is put into a glass of water until it will not dissolve any more. An equal quantity of indian ink is now added to it.

Another method as recommended by Lacourrière is to mix the contents of a tube of gamboge water-colour with one lump of French sugar (about two English lumps). No water is needed as the gamboge is very wet, but a little black gouache can be added to make it darker.

For the varnish, asphaltum with an equal quantity of turpentine is generally used. Another suggestion is to lay a thin hard ground over the plate which is supposed to lift easily.

How to make Plaster Prints without a Press

This is useful, particularly to someone who is on holiday, and who may want to see how an engraving is shaping. All that he needs is a tube of ink, scrim for cleaning, a sheet of glass and a bag of plaster of paris (fine dental plaster is the best).

The plate is inked up as if for printing in a press. It is then laid on the sheet of glass face upwards, and plaster is mixed into a bowl of water until it will not absorb any more and is beginning to heat up. It is then poured over the plate; it should be at least 1 in. thick. To contain the plaster it is a good plan to have previously made a 'frame' of four battens nailed together at the corners which is placed around the plate leaving a margin of an inch or two. When the plaster has set and cooled it is lifted off the glass and the plate gently removed with a knife at the corners.

It is now a three-dimensional object that can be hung on the wall or put on the mantelpiece, and if properly made will give a very perfect print of everything that is on the plate.

How to lay a Drawing on to a Hard Ground

For certain reasons it may be necessary to trace a drawing on to a hard ground, though this rather old-fashioned technique has been used in the past chiefly by those who treat etchings as reproductions of their drawings. It is clearly better to treat the drawing on the plate as an independent act. But there are occasions where it is important that a design should appear the right way round in the print, and here it is easy to put a reversed image of a pencil drawing down on to a hard ground that has been well smoked. The paper, preferably a smooth one, is wetted and laid carefully over the plate so that the design fits. It is then passed through the press with one blanket removed. The paper should come off easily, and even if some of it sticks, it will rub off with a little water leaving an impression of the drawing on the ground.

How to produce a 'Marbled Texture' (Illustration 50)

Flick some asphaltum on to the surface of a tray of water with a brush. Stir until the pattern pleases. Now carefully lower the surface of the bare plate to meet the water, where it should pick up the varnish. The plate is then stopped out and etched.

Dilute size instead of water may make the process easier.

Blake's method of Reverse Writing (Illustration 46)

Blake printed his *Prophetic Books* in relief etching from plates on which the text was written in reverse. It is inconceivable that he should have written everything the wrong way round, and scholars and artists have been concerned to know how he did it. Hayter has suggested a method that is fairly easy to do.

The writing is done with a fine brush in asphaltum diluted with turpentine (or benzine) to make it flow. It is written the right way round on a sheet of paper which has been previously coated with an equal mixture of gum arabic and soap. When the varnish is nearly, but not quite, dry, it is passed through the press over the plate which has been previously warmed. Afterwards the paper is soaked off, leaving the impression of the writing which may need a little correction here and there. It is then etched in weak nitric for several hours until sufficient relief has been obtained.

93

Some Sources of Etching Supplies

COMPILED WITH THE GUIDANCE OF THE PRATT GRAPHIC ART CENTER, NEW YORK

PRESSES
Bottega d'arte Grafica
Florence, Italy

Charles Brand
82 East 10 Street
New York, New York

Craftools, Inc.
1 Industrial Road
Wood-Ridge, New Jersey

Dickerson Combination
    Press
West Waubun Drive
Fontana, Wisconsin

G.A.C.E.P. Fratelli Paolini
Urbino, Italy

Hunter Penrose Ltd.
109 Farringdon Road
London EC1, England

Wilfred C. Kimber
    (Successors) Ltd
24 King's Bench Street
London SE1, England

Rembrandt Graphic Arts
    Co. Inc.
Stockton, New Jersey

Lee Sturges Etching Presses
Graphic Chemical and Ink
    Company
P.O. Box 27
Villa Park, Illinois

FELT BLANKETS
Aetna Felt Company Inc.
204 Center Street
New York, New York

The California Ink Company
2939 East Pico Boulevard
Los Angeles, California

Continental Felt Company
22-26 West 15 Street
New York 11, New York

TOOLS
Edward Lyons
64 Fulton Street
New York, New York

Craftools, Inc.
1 Industrial Road
Wood-Ridge, New Jersey

Graphic Chemical and Ink
    Company
P.O. Box 27
Villa Park, Illinois

M. Grumbacher
460 West 34 Street
New York, New York

Hunt Manufacturing
    Company
Box 560
Camden 1, New Jersey

Edward Lyons
64 Fulton Street
New York, New York

Frank Mittermeier
3577 East Tremont Avenue
Bronx 65, New York

Rembrandt Graphic Arts
    Company, Inc.
Stockton, New Jersey

F. Weber
1220 Buttonwood Street
Philadelphia, Pennsylvania

ROLLERS
Apex Printers' Roller
    Company
1541 North 16 Street
St. Louis 6, Missouri

Samuel Bingham's Son
    Manufacturing Company
364 9th Street
Jersey City, New Jersey

Craftools, Inc.
1 Industrial Road
Wood-Ridge, New Jersey

Ideal Rollers Company
21-24 39th Avenue
Long Island City, New York

GROUNDS, VARNISHES
Graphic Chemical and Ink
    Company
P.O. Box 27
Villa Park, Illinois

Craftools, Inc.
1 Industrial Road
Wood-Ridge, New Jersey

Harold M. Pitman
    Company
230 West 41 Street
New York, New York

PLATES
California Ink Company
2939 East Pico Boulevard
Los Angeles, California

Craftools, Inc.
1 Industrial Road
Wood-Ridge, New Jersey

Graphic Chemical and Ink
    Company
P.O. Box 27
Villa Park, Illinois

Harold M. Pitman
    Company
230 West 41 Street
New York, New York

Rembrandt Graphic Arts
    Company, Inc.
Stockton, New Jersey

ACIDS AND OTHER
    CHEMICALS
Graphic Chemical and Ink
    Company
P.O. Box 27
Villa Park, Illinois

S. Klenosky
543 Metropolitan Avenue
Brooklyn, New York

Harold M. Pitman
    Company
230 West 41 Street
New York, New York

Printer's Service, Inc.
225 South Street
New York, New York

Wholesale Supply Company
6500 Santa Monica
    Boulevard
Los Angeles, California

TARLATANS, RAGS
Beckmann Felt Company
120 Baxter Street
New York 13, New York

National Waste Company
366 Madison Avenue
New York 17, New York

ACID BATHS
Craftools, Inc.
1 Industrial Road
Wood-Ridge, New Jersey

Graphic Chemical and Ink
    Company
P.O. Box 27
Villa Park, Illinois

INKS
Charbonel
Quai Montebello
Paris 5e, France

Craftools, Inc.
1 Industrial Road
Wood-Ridge, New Jersey

Graphic Chemical and Ink
    Company
P.O. Box 27
Villa Park, Illinois

Hunt Manufacturing
    Company
Box 560
Camden 1, New Jersey

Kast-Echinger
Stuttgart-Feuerbach,
Germany

Harold M. Pitman
    Company
230 West 41 Street
New York, New York

Rembrandt Graphic Arts
    Company, Inc.
Stockton, New Jersey

F. Weber
1220 Buttonwood Street
Philadelphia, Pennsylvania

PAPER
Aiko's
714 North Wabash
Chicago 11, Illinois

Andrews-Nelson-
    Whitehead, Inc.
7 Laight Street
New York, New York

Crestwood Paper Company,
    Inc.
263 Ninth Avenue
New York 1, New York

STEEL FACING OF
    PLATES
Andersen-Lamb
48 Fulton Street
New York, New York

Index